COMPOSING AT THE PIANO

LEE EVANS MARTHA BAKER

PIANO

FUNCTIONAL SKILLS SERIES

Early Intermediate Level

CONTENTS

FOREWORD

While it is not imperative to have students complete the authors' previous composition book, "Learn To Compose and Notate Music at the Keyboard" (Beginning Level), a thorough understanding of the concepts and music-writing skills taught therein is nevertheless highly recommended.

All exercises should be played as well as written. When written, the teacher should instruct the student in such basics as stem direction (all stems down from the third staff line and above), the correct shape of rests, and the entering of dynamics and tempo markings in each piece where appropriate. A list of such recommended terms appear in the Glossary on page 16.

2nd Edition

Music Engravings and Typography by
Irwin Rabinowitz

Piano Plus, inc.

EXCLUSIVELY DISTRIBUTED BY
HAL•LEONARD® CORPORATION
7777 W. BLUEMOUND RD. P.O. BOX 13819 MILWAUKEE, WI 53213

INTRODUCTION and REVIEW

The authors' volume, "Learn To Compose and Notate Music" (Beginning Level), teaches four fundamental composing techniques — *repetition, sequence, retrograde,* and *inversion.* A brief definition and example of each of these follows:

Repetition means to repeat a motive (a musical theme) — note for note — starting on the same pitch.

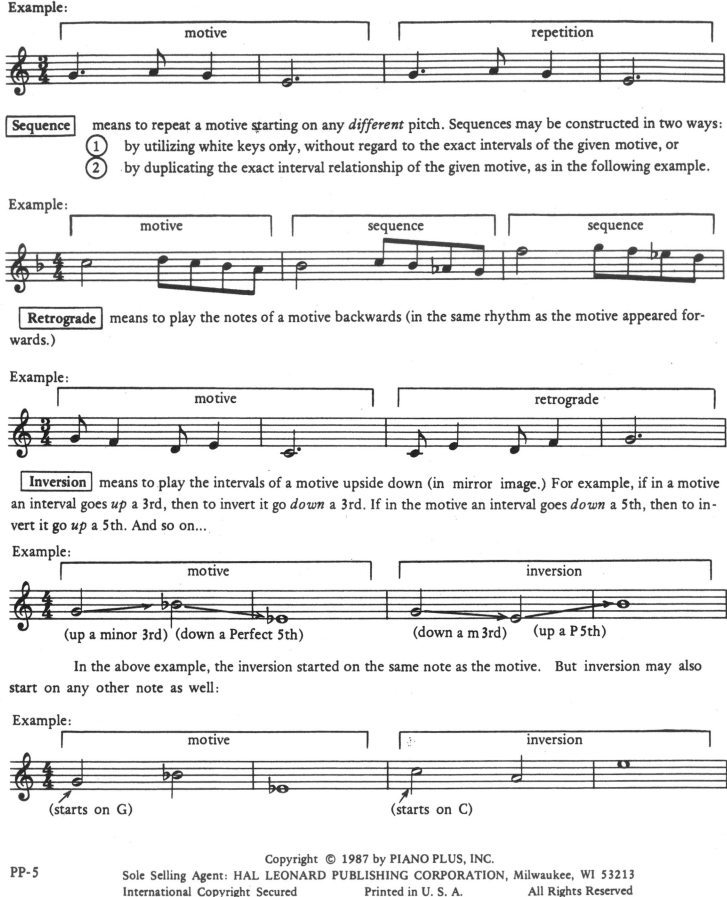

Sequence means to repeat a motive starting on any *different* pitch. Sequences may be constructed in two ways:

① by utilizing white keys only, without regard to the exact intervals of the given motive, or

② by duplicating the exact interval relationship of the given motive, as in the following example.

Retrograde means to play the notes of a motive backwards (in the same rhythm as the motive appeared forwards.)

Inversion means to play the intervals of a motive upside down (in mirror image.) For example, if in a motive an interval goes *up* a 3rd, then to invert it go *down* a 3rd. If in the motive an interval goes *down* a 5th, then to invert it go *up* a 5th. And so on...

In the above example, the inversion started on the same note as the motive. But inversion may also start on any other note as well:

LESSON 1

COMPOSING: OSTINATO

Ostinato means a short, constantly repeated musical phrase (motive), usually repeated at the same pitch, but not always.

Example:

The following is another example of an ostinato.

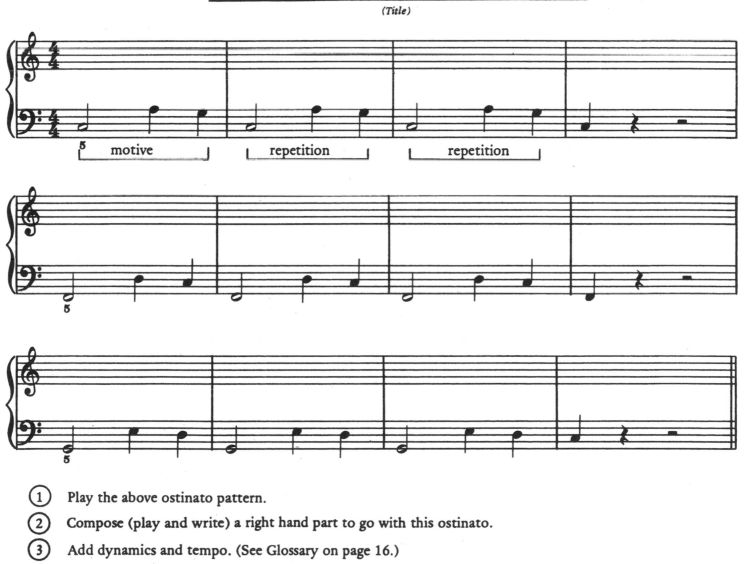

(1) Play the above ostinato pattern.

(2) Compose (play and write) a right hand part to go with this ostinato.

(3) Add dynamics and tempo. (See Glossary on page 16.)

(4) Give your composition a title in the space above.

(5) Practice this composition as part of your regular piano practice.

LESSON 2

COMPOSING: OSTINATO

Compose (play and write) your own ostinatos.

Use a different key signature for each ostinato.

Choose any time signature you wish.

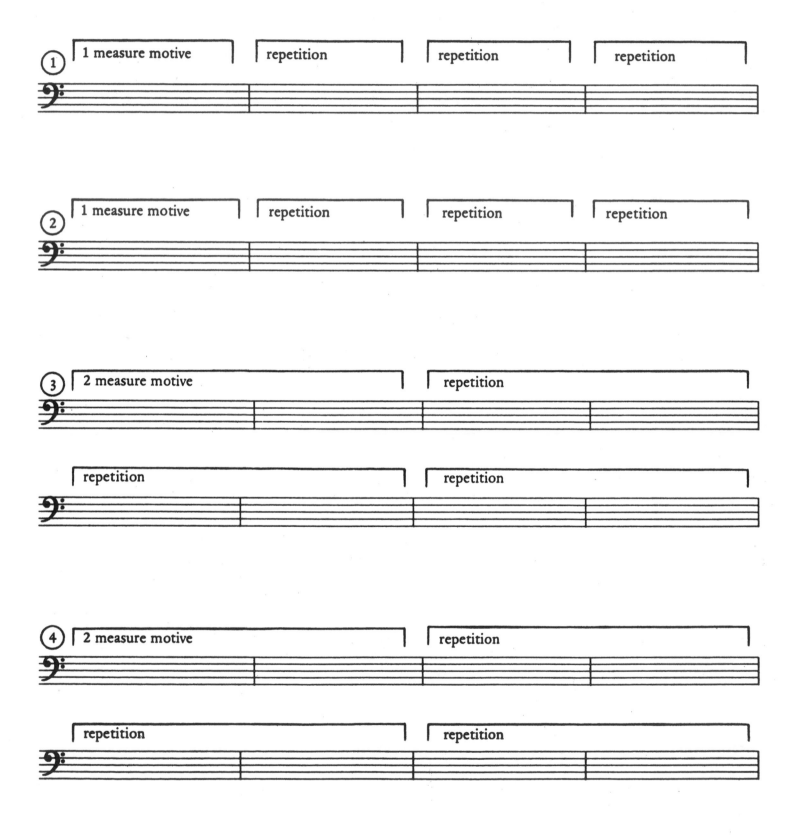

LESSON 3

COMPOSING: OSTINATO

1. Choose one of your one-measure motives from LESSON 2 and write it six times (measures 1 - 6) on the manuscript paper below. (Reminder: Enter key and time signatures.)

2. Play this ostinato pattern on the piano.

3. Compose (play and write) a right hand part to go with this ostinato.

4. Compose an ending for this piece in measures 7 and 8.

5. Give your composition a title in the space below.

6. Practice this composition as part of your regular piano practice.

Note: In order to make all your compositions sound final and complete, you may wish to consider ending with the tonic tone or tonic chord.

(Title)

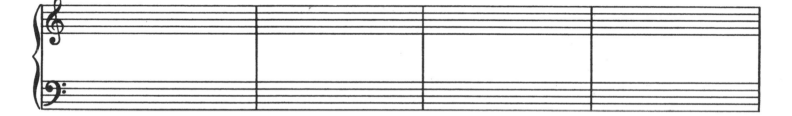

COMPOSING: OSTINATO

LESSON 4

1. Choose one of your two-measure motives from LESSON 2 and write it seven times (measures 1-14) on the manuscript paper below. (Reminder: Enter key and time signatures.)

2. Play this pattern on the piano.

3. Compose (play and write) a right hand part to go with this ostinato.

4. Compose an ending for this piece in measures 15 and 16.

5. Give your composition a title in the space below.

6. Practice this composition as part of your regular piano practice.

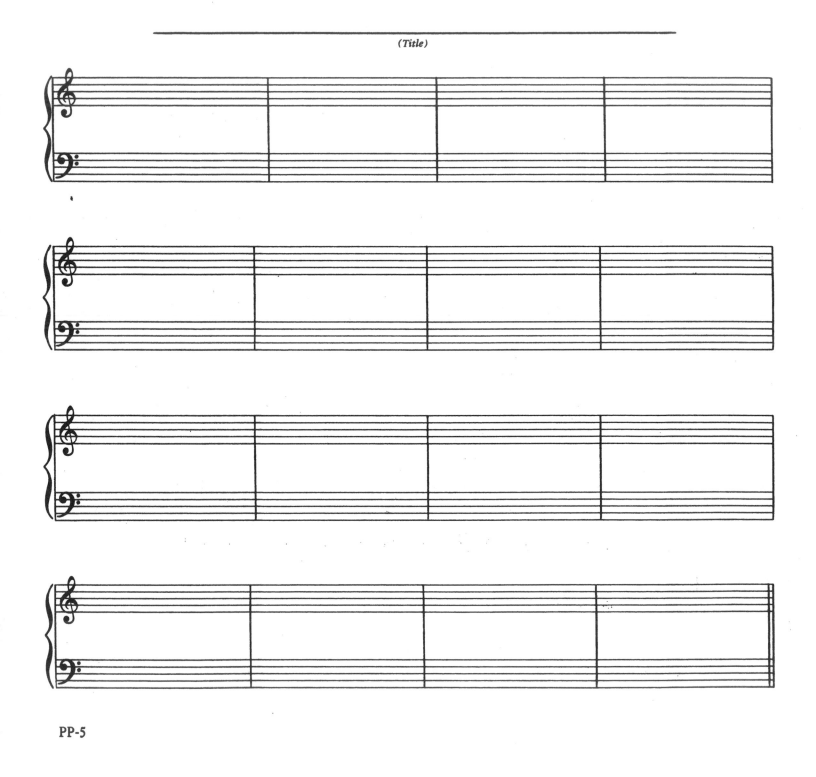

(Title)

COMPOSING: PEDAL POINT

LESSON 5

The compositional technique you have just learned (ostinato) features *constant repetition.* Another repetition technique used in composing is pedal point.

Pedal Point   means a constantly repeated musical tone or interval. A pedal tone or interval may appear in either treble or bass clef.

Play the following examples several times to hear the stationary (non-moving) quality of this compositional device, as the sounds (harmonies) move above or below it. Also notice that the end of each example sounds final (resolved) because each example ends on the tonic tone or tonic chord.

Pedal point in bass

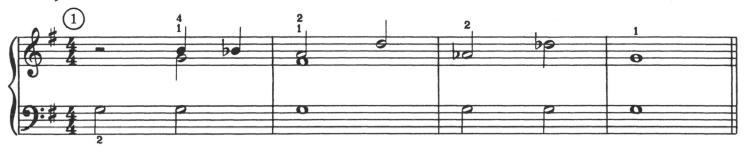

Pedal interval in treble

Compose your own four-measure examples below. Use two different key and time signatures.

Pedal point in treble

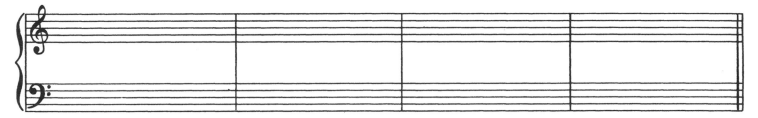

Pedal interval in bass

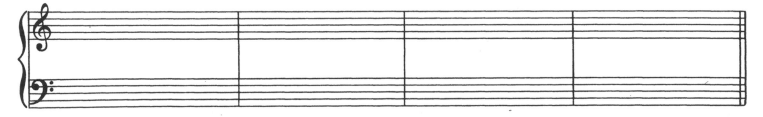

PP-5

COMPOSING: PEDAL POINT

LESSON 6

(1) Compose (play and write) your own eight measure composition.
Use *ostinato* in the first four measures and *pedal point* or *pedal interval* in the last four measures.
These compositional devices may be used in either the treble or bass clef.
(Reminder: Enter key and time signatures.)

_____
(Title)

(Ostinato)

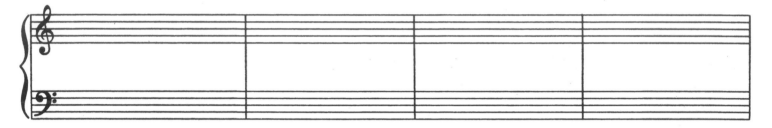

(Pedal point or pedal interval)

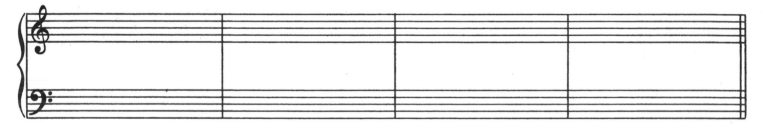

Resolution
(Final sound)

(2) Add dynamics and tempo.

(3) Give your composition a title in the space above.

(4) Practice this composition as part of your regular piano practice.

ALTERED FORMS OF SEQUENCE

LESSON 7

Good composers always vary their musical materials in order to create greater interest for the listener. For example, *sequence* is not always an exact repetition of a motive at another scale degree. Sequences may appear in altered forms such as *changing the rhythm*.

Examples:

① *Making the rhythms smaller:*

The melody stays the same, but note values become smaller.

② *Making the rhythms larger:*

The melody stays the same, but note values become larger.

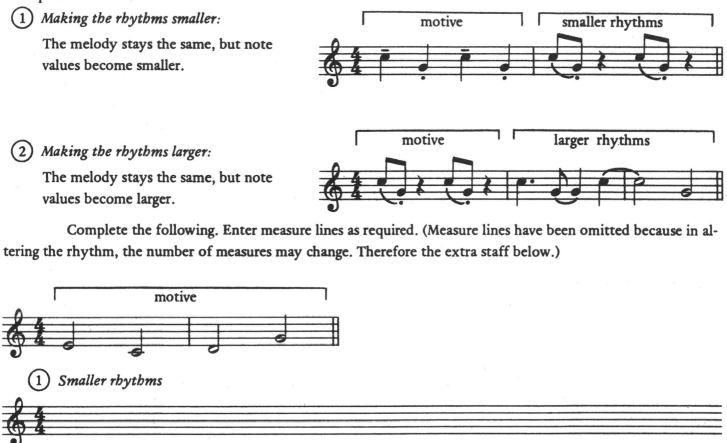

Complete the following. Enter measure lines as required. (Measure lines have been omitted because in altering the rhythm, the number of measures may change. Therefore the extra staff below.)

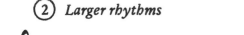

① *Smaller rhythms*

② *Larger rhythms*

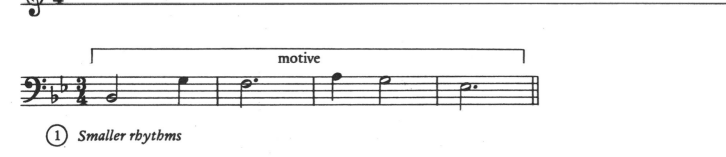

① *Smaller rhythms*

② *Larger rhythms*

ALTERED FORMS OF SEQUENCE

LESSON 8

Sequences may also appear in another kind of alteration, such as *changing the intervals.*

Examples:

① *Making the intervals smaller:*

The rhythm stays the same, but melodic intervals become smaller.

② *Making the intervals larger:*

The rhythm stays the same, but melodic intervals become larger.

Complete the following:

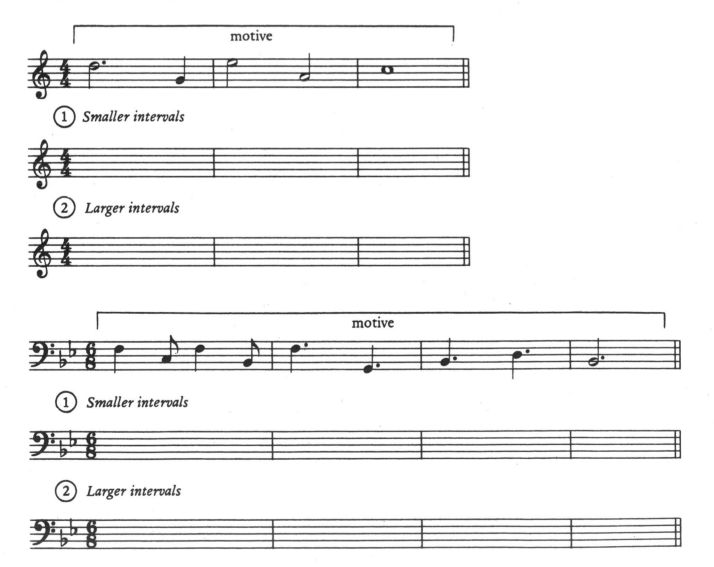

COMPOSING: ALTERED FORMS OF SEQUENCE

LESSON 9

① In the composition below, follow the directions in measures 3-8.

② After measure 8, make *smaller and larger rhythm changes* of the original right-hand motive to complete the piece. The left hand part throughout may be anything you want.

③ Draw bar lines as needed and a double bar at the end.

④ Add dynamics and tempo.

⑤ Give your composition a title.

⑥ Practice this composition as part of your regular piano practice.

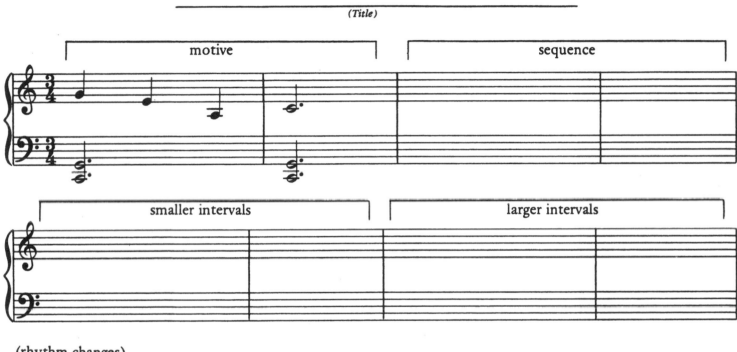

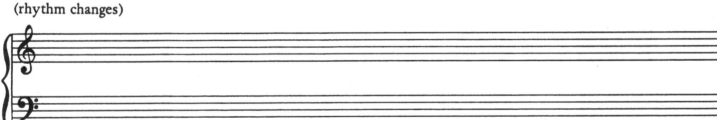

(rhythm changes)

COMPOSITIONAL ROUNDUP

LESSON 10

Create your own two-measure motive and compose a piece of any length, using the compositional devices of *larger rhythms, smaller rhythms, larger intervals,* and *smaller intervals.* In addition, you may use any or all of the other compositional devices you have learned so far.

First draw grand staffs, clefs and both key and time signatures. Add bar lines as needed, placing a double bar at the end of the composition. Include dynamics and tempo-markings. Give your composition a title.

_____
(Title)

FORM: 12 – BAR BLUES

LESSON 11

Too much repetition can result in music that is boring because it lacks *variety.* On the other hand, not enough repetition can result in music that lacks *unity* (the different parts sound as though they don't fit together.)

Composers often use certain musical forms to help provide a good balance between variety and unity in their music. One popular musical form which provides variety and unity is *12-bar blues.*

Variety in 12-bar blues comes partly from the use of several different chords — the I, IV and V chords — usually arranged in the following pattern:

12-bar blues

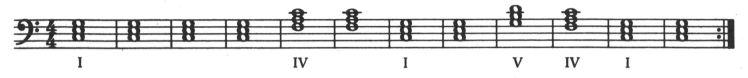

Play the above pattern several times with the left hand.

Unity in 12-bar blues is provided by two compositional devices with which you are already familiar — repetition and sequence — used often in this form, as shown below. (Keep in mind that sequence is repetition, but starting on a different pitch.)

12-bar blues

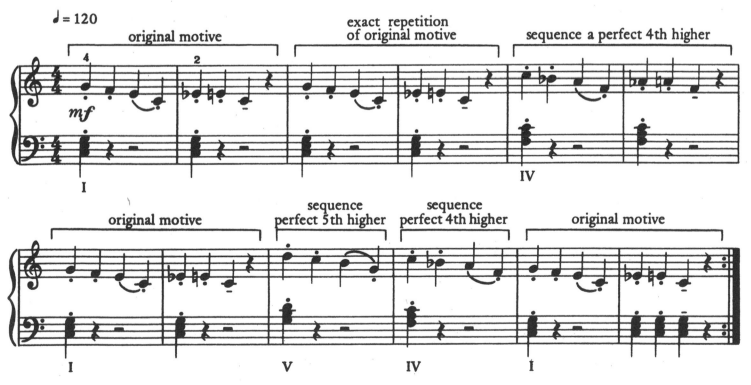

Practice the above blues composition as part of your regular piano practice, making sure to observe all staccato and phrase marks carefully.

COMPOSING: 12-BAR BLUES

LESSON 12

Use *repetition* and *sequence* to compose a 12-bar blues starting with the following 2-measure phrase.
Use the same left hand bass pattern throughout.

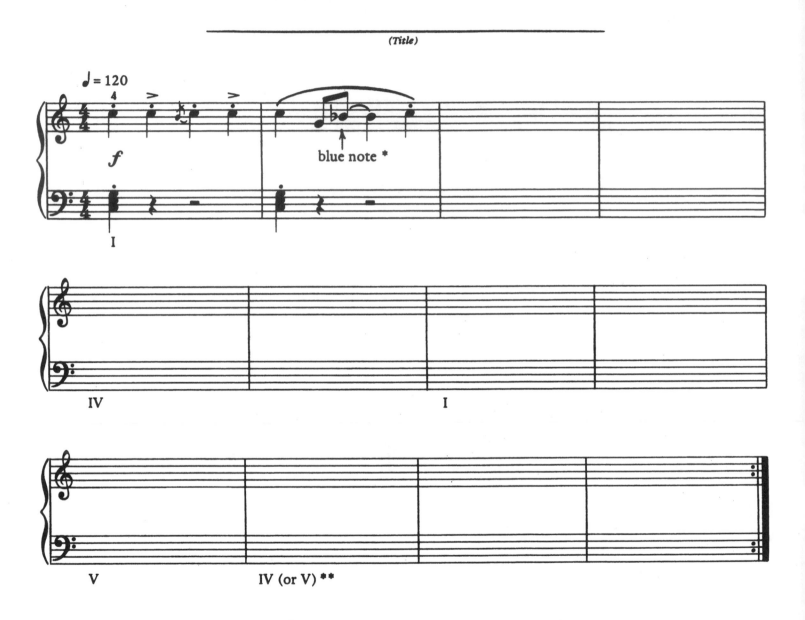

Give your composition a title in the space above. Practice this composition as part of your regular piano
practice.

* "Blue notes" are flatted 3rd, 5th and 7th degrees of the major scale. The blue note in measure 2 is a flatted 7th.

** The V chord is often substituted for the IV chord in bar 10 of the blues in order to accomodate the melodic line,
if necessary.

COMPOSING: 12-BAR BLUES

LESSON 13

Enter a key signature and time signature below. Then compose a two-measure motive for the right hand, using any bass pattern of your choice. Next, complete this blues composition according to the chord arrangement described in lessons 11 and 12.

Hint: The use of staccatos, accents on weak beats, and "blue notes" (♭3, ♭5, ♭7) will give your composition a stronger jazz effect.

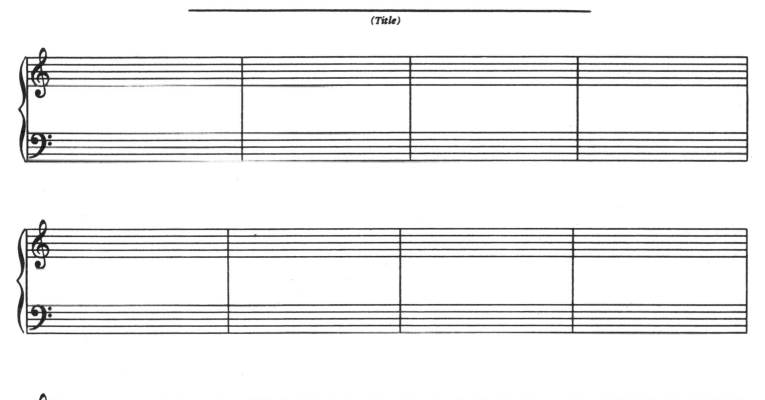

(Title)

Give your composition a title in the space above. Practice this composition as part of your regular piano practice.

You are now ready to proceed to Lee Evans' volume, *"Improvise By Learning How To Compose"* (Intermediate Level).

GLOSSARY

| Dynamic Markings: | | |

Abbreviation	*Italian*	*Definition*
pp	pianissimo	very soft
p	piano	soft
mf	mezzo forte	medium loud
f	forte	loud
>	_____	accent
(crescendo hairpin)	crescendo	gradually louder
(diminuendo hairpin)	diminuendo (decrescendo)	gradually softer

| Tempo Markings: | |

Italian	*Definition*
Lento	slow
Andante	medium slow
Moderato	medium tempo
Allegro	medium fast; happy
Vivace	fast; lively
Rubato	elasticity and freedom of tempo, with slight accelerandos and ritardandos

Italian tempo markings are not ordinarily employed in jazz. Instead, it is recommended that jazz and blues compositions use such simple but descriptive phrases as:

With a driving beat	Swing feel
Steadily	With a lift
Brightly	Rhythmically
Moderately bright	Expressively
Moderate swing tempo	Easy ballad tempo
Medium bounce	Slow blues feel
Bounce tempo	Move it!

A metronome mark following any one of these terms is also useful.

Example: Medium bounce (♩ = 126)